D0754718

Bilingual Edition

Let's Draw with Shapes™

Edición Bilingüe

Let's Draw a
Bear with Squares

Vamos a dibujar un
oso usando cuadrados

Kathy Kuhtz Campbell
Illustrations by Emily Muschinske

Traduccion al español:
María Cristina Brusca

The Rosen Publishing Group's
PowerStart Press™ & **Editorial Buenas Letras**™
New York

Published in 2004 by The Rosen Publishing Group, Inc.
29 East 21st Street, New York, NY 10010

First Edition

Book Design: Emily Muschinske

Photo Credits: Photograph of bears on pp. 23, 24 Kennan Ward/CORBIS.

Campbell, Kathy Kuhtz
        Let's draw a bear with squares = Vamos a dibujar un oso usando cuadrados /
Kathy Kuhtz Campbell ; illustrations by Emily Muschinske ; translated by María Cristina Brusca.
                p. cm. — (Let's draw with shapes)
        Includes index.
        Summary: This book offers simple instructions for using squares to draw a bear.
        ISBN 1-4042-7501-0 (lib.)
        1. Bears in art—Juvenile literature   2. Drawing—Technique—Juvenile literature
[1. Bears in art   2. Drawing—Technique   3. Spanish language materials—Bilingual]   I.
Muschinske, Emily   II. Title   III. Series
        NC655 C3563 2004   2003-009167
        743.6—dc21

Manufactured in the United States of America

Due to the changing nature of Internet links, PowerStart Press has developed an online list of Web sites related to the subject of this book. This site is updated regularly. Please use this link to access the list:

http://www.buenasletraslinks.com/ldwsh/oso

2

Contents

Contenido

3

Draw a red square to begin your bear.

Comienza tu oso dibujando un cuadrado rojo.

Draw a small orange square for the head of your bear.

Dibuja un pequeño cuadrado anaranjado, para hacer la cabeza de tu oso.

7

Add a yellow square for the tummy of your bear.

Agrega un cuadrado amarillo, para hacer la panza de tu oso.

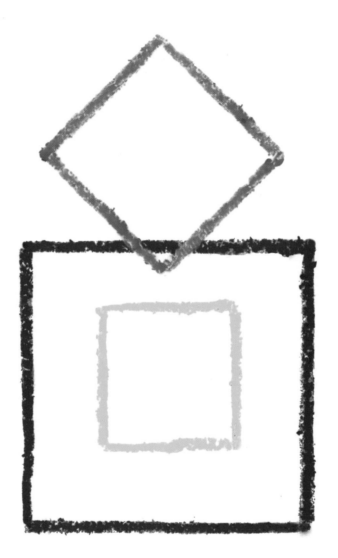

9

Draw two little green squares
for the ears of your bear.

Dibuja dos pequeños
cuadrados verdes,
para hacer las orejas
de tu oso.

Draw one blue square for each paw of your bear.

Dibuja un cuadrado azul por cada una de las patas delanteras de tu oso.

Draw two purple squares for two more paws.

Dibuja dos cuadrados violeta para hacer las otras dos patas.

15

Draw three small black squares for the face of your bear.

Dibuja tres pequeños cuadrados negros, para hacer la cara de tu oso.

Color in your bear.

Colorea tu oso.

This mother bear has two babies called cubs.

Esta mamá osa tiene dos bebés llamados oseznos.

Words to Know / Palabras que debes saber

cubs
oseznos

ears
orejas

paw
pata

Colors / Colores

 red / rojo

 orange / anaranjado

yellow / amarillo

 green / verde

blue / azul

purple / violeta

pink / rosa

black / negro

Index

Índice